POWERFUL
TECHNIQUES FOR EFFECTIVE SUBCONSCIOUS COMMUNICATION

THE ADVANTAGE YOU NEED TO SUCCEED

JAY MAYMI

7 POWERFUL TECHNIQUES FOR EFFECTIVE SUBCONSCIOUS COMMUNICATION – *THE ADVANTAGE YOU NEED TO SUCCEED*
Copyright © 2018 by Jay Maymi

All rights reserved. Printed in the United States of America. No part of this book may be used or reproduced in any manner whatsoever without written permission except in the case of brief quotations embodied in critical articles or reviews.

For information contact:
http://www.thejaymaymi.com

Book and Cover design by Ivette Maymi
ISBN 978-0-9915419-2-8

First Edition: March 2018
Reprint: January 2019

POWERFUL
TECHNIQUES FOR EFFECTIVE SUBCONSCIOUS COMMUNICATION

THE ADVANTAGE YOU NEED TO SUCCEED

JAY MAYMI

CONTENTS

REVIEWS 1

INTRODUCTION 5

TECHNIQUE 1 9

TECHNIQUE 2 17

TECHNIQUE 3 21

TECHNIQUE 4 29

TECHNIQUE 5 37

TECHNIQUE 6 43

TECHNIQUE 7 49

TECHNIQUE 8 53

TECHNIQUE 9 61

TECHNIQUE 10 67

CLOSING 71

ABOUT THE AUTHOR 73

A WORD FROM JAY MAYMI 75

REVIEWS

"This book teaches you how to communicate directly with a person's subconscious mind to influence them more effectively. I highly recommend it."

Steve Siebold, *Author*
"Secrets Self-Made Millionaires Teach Their Kids"

"Jay does a masterful job of taking something so complex and powerful as the subconscious mind and dialing into the basic techniques that can transform anyone's sales career or improve their relationships. Following his simple yet powerful strategies can take anyone from a novice to a master in a relatively short period of time and drastically increase their results! An absolute must read."

Chris Felton, *Co-Author*
"Couples Money"

"My compliments to Jay Maymi for taking what can be a complex skill to achieve and making it seem easy and attainable. In my 20+ years in the legal and financial industries, I've seen many professionals (myself included at times), "try too hard" to win the business or build a relationship with colleagues, clients and prospects. Eagerness can often crush good intent. I love Jay's direct and no-nonsense approach to coaching. He understands the challenges professionals, as well as all individuals, face when trying to be relate-able and thereby successful. His seven techniques are things that anyone can master if they focus and continue to try to improve. After I achieve all my goals, I plan to write a thank you to Jay Maymi."

Charlsey Baumeier
National Business Development Officer

"Effort alone does not create success. Somebody can put forth a lifetime of effort and not have much to show for it. 'Outstanding accomplishment and disappointing mediocrity are both built from the same 24 hours in each day.' The system for most is fundamentally flawed and broken. We all have the same 24 hours. The real difference is what you decide to do with it. Jay Maymi's new book will help you develop the wisdom and skills necessary to move you from being a push over to a mountain mover. Each chapter provides a key to help you unlock the vault of abundance and live Life Unlimited. Buy it, read it, apply it and you'll move from just enough to More Than Enough.

Kevin Mullens, *Pastor, Speaker, Global Business Builder (Zija), 4x Author, Movie Producer*

"Easily read in less than an hour, the content in '**7 Powerful Techniques for Effective Subconscious Communication**' is nevertheless very impactful. I can attest from personal experience that the communication skills taught in this book are extremely effective. The chapter about names alone is worth the time and money investment. You'll benefit by having this book in your personal library!"

Bob Sager, *Author*
"Discovering Your Greatness: A Higher-Level Thinking and Action Guide"

"Jay truly packs a punch with his latest book. In simple steps, Jay teaches us how to communicate better with others in a more effective way. An indispensable skill to develop. This book a must training tool."

Adeline Ortiz, *Founder and CEO*
Rising Phoenix Center for Law and Politics

INTRODUCTION

My life, work, and entrepreneurial experiences so far have taught me that if you are going to be in the people business then you'd better understand how people think and what makes them tick. After all, what separates a novice communicator from one whose effectiveness is at *ninja status* or *mastery mode* is simply what he or she can draw out of the person they are communicating with. The ambitious yet novice sales person, negotiator, marketer, entrepreneur, or anyone for that matter who interacts with others for a living must understand that there is another level of communication that exists and if incorporated properly can produce wonderful results in whatever pursuit they are undertaking. Quite frankly, attempting to be successful without mastering these skills or accessing these available tactics is equivalent to going to combat with one arm tied behind your back, or stepping up to the baseball plate to face a 90 MPH fastball pitcher with a whiffle ball bat. Are you getting the picture? There is no way you can expect to be as effective as you can be under those circumstances. Simply put, if you are going to strive to be the best that you can be at whatever you are pursuing then don't sell yourself short. Embrace the fact that there are higher laws of communication available other than what your five senses provide. There is a major advantage in going past the conscious mind of an individual and penetrating their subconscious to increase the probability of a desired action from that individual.

Now, let me stop here for a moment to clear the air. I do not endorse techniques that are intended for wrongful manipulation or misappropriation. Clearly, the application of morality, ethics, and honesty must be applied here. However, when utilized properly and with right intentions you do find that the end results are two parties who have come to a mutually beneficial agreement and relationship.

The bottom line is that your increased effectiveness as a communicator may be the very thing that the other person requires you to be to help guide them. If you sincerely believe in the goodness of what you do, then using effective subconscious communication techniques can become the defining difference in the amount of people you ultimately help and the lives you change for the better. Personally, I can attest that having utilized these techniques after being made aware of them due to an extensive career in sales, academic studies, research projects, and numerous workshops in sales psychology for over 25 years, that they've made a profound difference in my business, career, and life. I am very confident that they will do the same for you.

One final point. Although I could have taken a much more intensive academic and scientific approach to this book (considering my background experiences in the fields of psychology, social work, counseling, human behavior, and sales psychology and marketing), I decided it was not called for. This is lay literature. Besides, thinking like most busy people, I wanted to trim the fat, cut to the chase, and just deliver the applicable nuts and bolts stuff. I know that's how I think and I'm sure most busy go-getters think the same way. Even though, I will cover some minor aspects of Psychology, Sociology, and Biology, my intent is to keep it light in these areas and focus more on the day to day application of these very powerful and effective subconscious communication techniques.

1

"First...Just a little Biology and Psychology"

As we dive into a training like this it is vital that you first have a working understanding of the brain (biology) and the mind or consciousness (psychology). Having a grasp of the basic functions of the different parts of the brain and how it is affected by the workings of the mind will make comprehension of this book as well as the application of these techniques much more effective. The brain, even though a 3 pound, grey and firm jelly-like matter, is the most important organ in our body. It consists of three main parts:

1.   **Cerebrum**. This major (and largest) part of the brain is involved in remembering, problem solving, thinking, and feeling, as well as controlling movement. It fills up most of the skull.

2.   **Cerebellum**. This part of the brain controls coordination and balance and sits at the back of your head under the cerebrum.

3.   **Brain stem**. This part of the brain also known as Reptilian brain or "old brain" because it is the oldest and innermost region of the brain. It connects the brain to the spinal cord and controls automatic functions such as breathing, digestion, heart rate and blood pressure. It regulates basic survival functions and creates our experiences of emotions. One of the main areas of function that is important for us to understand for the purpose of this book is that the old brain also serves in protection by the awareness of danger. Keep in mind that in early developmental life we were not as complex beings as we are now. Generally, we had only

one purpose and it was not to create the world's next technological toy, end world hunger, design better cars, and so on. Our only purpose was to survive. That's all the old brain was designed to do. It wasn't until later in our human evolution that the brain developed further as the need for higher functioning and thought demanded it. Why is this piece of information so instrumental for subconscious mind communication? Because the "old brain" has not forgotten it's first and main assignment: survival.

Now, let's explore the mind. As easy as it was to provide for you a straightforward and basic breakdown of the three main parts of the brain, the mind offers no such luck. In fact, anyone who tries to define the mind with assured accuracy is traveling a slippery path. The concept of mind continues to evolve in the scientific and psychological communities. The one belief that is generally accepted is that the mind is the seat of consciousness and the essence of our being and without it you are not pointedly alive. In fact, consciousness for us is all there is. Without it, there is no recognition of self, there is no experience of joy and suffering, no world. There is basically nothing. The scientific community has traditionally explained mind as brain activity, however, continuing studies and a growing body of evidence points to the realization that the mind is much more. Scientists from all disciplines are always studying consciousness and trying to understand the properties of this complex mystery even further. Therefore, it is an ever-developing field of study that will continue to bring about new understanding as time passes.

For this training book what is most relevant to know is that your experiences, emotions, thoughts, focus, memories, self-organization, and mental programming are all part of the mind. The next concept to know is that there are essentially 2 levels of the mind that work together to bring about our reality: the conscious and subconscious (interchangeable with unconscious) as popularized by the Austrian psychologist Sigmund Freud. Even though the general notion of conscious and subconscious have been around for hundreds, if not thousands of years. It wasn't until Freud gave it practical significance that it was popularized. This tiered [level] mind concept has been hotly debated in the scientific, psychological, and philosophical circles ever since because it has been very hard to prove, empirically. However, as the debate continues, many studies, research, and programs have proven successful when utilizing this tier approach to consciousness. It has also served to help millions of people in therapeutic, personal development, business, academic, military, and social agendas. Let's briefly examine how it all works.

Your conscious mind acts much like the Captain of a ship. The Captain stands on the bridge giving orders to the crew but that is all he or she does. The crew below are the ones directing where the ship is going. The Captain relays to the crew the external information that the crew cannot observe because they are below deck. The crew, upon receiving this information, then acts according to what they know to do from past experiences or training. Similarly, the conscious mind (figuratively speaking, Captain) transmits external information to the subconscious mind (again, figuratively speaking, the crew) based on what it sees, smells, feels, and hears. The subconscious mind takes this information and begins to act accordingly. The subconscious mind is the storehouse of everything we have experienced since birth, although many believe that it can go even further back to days in the womb. Every memory that we have, whether suppressed on purpose, repressed by trauma, or simply forgotten is recorded in the subconscious mind. Our deep-rooted beliefs, habits, and behaviors are formed from these stored experiences and memories.

For the sake of the most practical application of this information the key takeaway is to understand that the reality we experience comes, just as much, from how we process external influences and data as it does from how we process the existing internal one as well. Our subconscious mind can help orchestrate a new reality based on stored data and beliefs or from developing new ones when presented with new information. In other words, from the inside we can create what happens on the outside. Most of our decisions are made at the subconscious level. This is where it originates so why not learn to communicate effectively with it? To provide another parallel example that we can all relate to, let's look at your computer. Whether it is a desktop, laptop, even a cell phone, you have the hard drive which is the physical component containing wiring, boards, operating systems, simple pre-installed software, etc. Without any additional or significant programing installed or downloaded, it is just a well-engineered and designed object. It does not know what actions it should process. You can turn on the power and get a lovely bright screen image but that's about it. However, when you begin to install programs and software that's when it becomes functional. Your computer system will react to the request you ask of it only when it already has that programming installed.

So, essentially everything begins at the programming level. This is where it becomes truly operational and useful. Our brain acts like an organic computer. It contains all the necessary "hard wiring" called neurons which the subconscious mind transmits messages and instructions to the brain which creates human functionality. However, without the mind and its programming there is very little achievement that can occur past the basic living functions. The software that is installed in the mind will have a lot to do with what kind of experience you have, and this is where it gets interesting. It is important to remember that the subconscious mind acts like a memory bank which produces reactions, emotions, beliefs, and feelings when faced with familiar situations. As one who seeks to master the skill of effective communication, persuasion, and impression, this is tremendously advantageous to know and incorporate as you will see moving ahead.

2

"A Word about Words"

Barring a traumatic or tragic event or accident, there are a number of less traumatizing means that exist which can alter a person's mood, countenance, physiology, emotions, and mental faculty almost immediately. Drugs, alcohol, and chemical substances certainly can. A picture of an event or a person can have the same effect to a milder extent. Even an odor or scent can elicit an altering as well. However, none of these can be so effective in completely changing someone's mood, thoughts, perspective, and attitude in addition to the aforementioned effects quite like the words one hears. Words require no ingestion of drugs, alcohol, or chemical substances nor do they require a certain scent or need for sight. They simply require the ears to hear them and the mind to process them and off we go. Therefore, words are the most powerful resource you have at your disposal to build someone up or tear them down. It is why we find a Scripture verse in the Bible which states that "life and death is found in the power of the tongue". Words have the capacity to pierce through the conscious part of our mind and penetrate the subconscious like nothing else. They can become like the rudders on a ship and direct the rest of the mind and body where to go, what to do, and how to react. By the way, whether they are words that you hear from an outside source or words that you speak from your own mouth, they will take root in your subconscious mind and begin to produce either crab grass or a beautiful bed of flowers on the landscape of your subconscious mind.

For example, words that serve to compliment, criticize, or curse can often take a bee line to the center of someone's mind and draw forth reactions not present just a few seconds prior. It is quite amazing how a simple collection of letters can carry so much weight in directing another person's entire being almost instantaneously. When used properly, this provides the communicator with tremendous leverage and power.

Finally, words can serve as agents of cognitive pre-framing. This means that when used effectively and strategically, they can be quite effective in directing the mind of another person. This tactful approach can help you position the mind to cooperate with the thoughts or feelings you are looking to attract from them. Understanding how the subconscious can react to certain words starts one's journey from novice communicator to one at the level of master.

The rest of this book will focus on which words and phrases become the most effective when beginning to communicate with another person's subconscious mind and why. I will be providing sample phrases or examples when appropriate to illuminate the point I'll be making about that technique.

Ready? Fantastic! Now, I want you to imagine....

3

Technique #1
"The Imagine Directive"

Here is a truth. Our minds have the capacity to produce more elaborate visions, cinematography, and dream sequences than any Hollywood movie or CGI expert can ever produce. In fact, it doesn't take much for the human mind to create a full-length feature film just off one thought, idea, or even a word. I'm sure most of you can personally attest to this truth based on your own experiences.

Can you recall the many times that you have "spaced out" for a moment simply because you had a quick thought that evolved into a movie trailer? Or something or someone that momentarily caught your eye happened to take hold of your mind and keep you captive to the next few thoughts that entered it? In fact, once you become aware that you've "checked out" momentarily you're amazed at how subtle it was and how so many thoughts came so fast in such a small window of time. The mind is ready at the helm to take flight into the world of fantasy and imagery at every opportunity given.

Now, this can be a healthy thing if controlled and properly channeled, or incredibly detrimental to your professional progress and success if not managed. For this technique, a subconscious mind that is ready at the helm to take imaginary flight can be very advantageous to the advanced communicator who is trying to pre-pave the other person's mind to his point of view or persuasion. A powerful technique here becomes giving the other person the directive or instruction to "IMAGINE". Yes, to imagine. Here's how it works.

The conscious mind, being the predominant faculty responsible for reason and calculations, cannot imagine as well or nearly to the degree that the subconscious mind can. The subconscious looks for opportunities to exercise its imagination. When given instruction or directive to do so, it complies immediately. In fact, once you give another person the directive to "IMAGINE", the subconscious cannot avoid doing it. You cannot stop the subconscious mind from beginning to imagine the very thing that you have instructed it to do. Let's put this to the test, shall we?

I want you to imagine that a passenger plane carrying 240 passengers and crew just crashed in the ocean. Can you imagine that? I bet you did with 100% certainty. Why? I gave your subconscious mind a directive to imagine. Did you catch that? Now, be honest. The minute I gave you the instruction or directive you could not NOT have imagined a plane crashing into the ocean, true? Well, the minute you started to imagine it, I began communicating with your subconscious mind and thereby giving me tremendous access and leverage to persuade. Let me give you another example to continue highlighting this very crucial technique that has the potential to radically improve your communication abilities and success. Ready? I want you to imagine that it is dead of summer, the weather is humid, hot, and hazy. Can you imagine that? Then, imagine that you are running a long-distance marathon in the heat and there hasn't been a water station for 2 miles. Can you imagine just how thirsty you would be?

Now, I don't know about you but even as I was writing this and imagining it I was getting thirsty and guess what? I had to stop typing and go to the water cooler and get a drink of water and I wasn't even thirsty 2 minutes ago! How many of you either did the same thing or are feeling a little parched or dry mouth right now? You see? It works, doesn't it? Why does it work? It works because your subconscious mind doesn't know what's real or not. It just takes a thought or directive and believes it to be true and sends signals to the conscious mind to act in the way it would if it were true. In this case, convincing the conscious mind that you're thirsty. The conscious mind reacts to those instructions by telling the body, "Hey, get up and drink some water." Are you following? Did I lose anybody? It is incredibly important that you grasp this effective technique. It is about changing the way a person feels or sees a certain thing and take action that they may not have taken otherwise. One final example near and dear to my heart. It is dealing with expressing the importance to another individual concerning the need for life insurance. Now, I am using life insurance as the subject, but you can use whatever service, product, or opportunity you feel your potential client should engage in.

"Jackie, I want you to imagine (pause and give the subconscious mind a moment to go on alert) for a moment getting the worst call or visit that a wife can ever receive giving you the tragic news that your husband and father of your children is deceased. Imagine (pause) how your life will be turned upside down emotionally let alone financially if there isn't a means to replace the income that you will continue to need to raise your children. As hard as this is to imagine, these things do happen, don't they?" By the way, the second she answers who now has leverage? I do. Can you see that?

Powerful isn't it? Could Jackie not imagine this scenario? It would be hard to do, especially the part about getting the call or visit. As difficult as it would be to imagine it, or no matter how much she would resist, she would not be able to stop her subconscious from bringing forth that imagery and hence the accompanying feelings that would follow. Are you starting to get this? The reality is that the reason why the subconscious mind can be so easily communicated with, and effortlessly persuaded, is because the more common the imaginative directive the more the subconscious accepts it as true and fires off vibrations that evolve into constructive thoughts, feelings, and action.

Let me make just one final point on this. There are other similar words | phrases that certainly can conjure up the same effects. Words | phrases like:

"envision",
"visualize",
"picture this",
"I want you to make a mental picture of", and
"I want you to see in your mind"

These varying directives also achieve the same result. However, the word imagine is still the most potent. It has the greatest potential to alter the other person's entire mood and perspective, thereby creating a more welcoming reception to your offer or recommendation. When constructed properly in a sentence and delivered with good form, it will create for you a powerful method to circumvent the conscious mind and penetrate deep into the inner chambers of the subconscious.

Technique #2
"The Power of Social Alliances"

We were not fashioned to be lone beings. It is against our social design to live a life completely alone and without human interaction especially in group dynamics. It is extremely rare that you will find someone who has completely isolated themselves from the world and from any other human contact. Unless that individual has experienced hurt because of human contact and has resolved to withdraw to a life of isolation, most humans crave and need connection. As any other primate seeks group affiliation so do we. This is why through human history we find tribes, clans, associations, clubs, memberships and so on of every possible kind and for every possible reason. From volunteer groups to churches, from annual family reunions to business teams, we are always looking to become a part of something that can give us what we all desire deep down inside...a sense of belonging. This sense of belonging is what drives people to join things whether for good intentions or not. In a healthy group setting, or what I like to call "a like-minded alliance", people feel safe, secure, understood, and valued. A measure of comfort exists in this environment because of the familiarity of the setting, the content, and the other people in that group. There is less risk of hurt in an environment that is welcoming. This is exactly what the mind at the subconscious level seeks to provide instinctively - safety, security, protection, and survival. Are you starting to get the picture yet? When you speak to the subconscious mind about such things it will have your full attention because it complies with its innate survival laws. As we have mentioned, if one of the purposes of the subconscious mind or the primitive mind is survival, then anything that will resemble this it will receive without resistance. The opposite, therefore, exists as well. If the subconscious mind perceives that there is danger or potential for harm, it will provide several psychological and physiological transmissions to the conscious mind to stay away. Here is a simple test that will prove my point.

If you receive a call today from a friend who asks you if you would be willing to be a well-paid participant as target practice for the local beginners Knife Throwers Club's next meeting, you would probably give a two-part answer, "HELL NO!" Right? Unless, of course, you like courting pain and death. The subconscious mind would hear that request and immediately deem it as potentially life threatening and within milliseconds generate a response congruent with its natural intent to protect the body from hurt and preserve life.

On the other hand, if you received a call about volunteering with a group of neighbors to support the local senior citizens home you would probably respond by saying "yes". Why? Apart from being an act of kindness, it is deemed as not life threatening or harmful to you so the subconscious gives it a green light. Is this making sense to you?

We wonder sometimes why people are so quick to say no to an offer that would bring them value, life change and enhancement, a new experience, more money, better health, deeper relationships, yet not realizing all the dynamics that are happening in the backdrop that may have had a large part in that person declining your proposition. So, knowing this incredible piece of information allows you to effectively communicate with another person's subconscious mind recognizing that there are really two dynamics at play here for this technique: social and psychological. You effectively communicate using your words and imagery. Since words are your first and most powerful resource, using words that speak of a "like minded alliance" will automatically surface the same imagery and feelings that the individual already has programmed as a result of belonging to some other "like-minded alliance". This can be a social group, church, fraternity or organization. It is any association or alliance that they are part of that is safe, warm, loving, peaceful, fun, uplifting and supportive.

In other words, capitalize on the pre-existing experience that the subconscious is holding because of being a part of another group. Make the best use of the wiring that is already in place from either a current or previous pleasant experience. If one does not exist, then create one with your words. Let me give you a few examples below.

Sample #1

Note:

First you must ask a pre-paving question to determine if they are a part of any like-minded alliance (I cover what pre-paving questions are in my book Recruiting Mastery). If you know they are then skip this step. If not, then you must find out.

"April, can I ask you if you belong to any volunteer group or attend a local church?"

Note:
The second they answer, the work has begun because the mind is recalling the place or group and tapping into mental history and the accompanying feelings. It would be good to do a little prying here so that you can, not only, extract those memories, emotions, and overall sense of well-being from the recesses of that individual's subconscious mind but also to give you a little leverage with this technique.

"What is it about that group, church, etc. that you enjoy? Why do belong to them?"

Now the subconscious is primed for your next instruction.

"April, I ask because I belong to a group (team,

company, initiative, campaign, etc.) that shares a lot of the same values that are important to you. In fact, some of us have known each other for years and have been there through ups and downs. I'd love to have you join us the next time we get together."

Sample #2

"Hey Amber, a group of us are getting together for coffee and just have fun and talk. I'd love to introduce you to some of my friends. We're a great group of people."

Sample # 3

"Bill, our team is made up of incredible people that really support each other."

Sample # 4

"Alan, the reason why our organization continues to expand is because we have a bunch of people that really are like family and care for one another."

Sample # 5

"Around here we look after each other and love each other like family."

Sample #6

"When you get to know us, you'll feel like you've known us forever."

Now, a few things to keep in mind. This technique appeals to the natural social tendencies that we all have so do not infuse anything that is too heavy or burdensome. Keep it light and focus on the basic human need of belonging. This technique is very effective when you are looking to begin establishing a relationship with someone new that you've just met. Or, bring them around an environment that they can feel good returning to again and again. The person who might be initially resistant to attending some corporate meeting or stuffy presentation may have a change of heart once they bond with the people who are part of the group.

5

Technique #3 (Part 1)
"Terms of Social Endearment"

Have you ever felt an immediate bond with someone within minutes of meeting and/or speaking with them? It is almost as if you've known them for a long time. There is something about them that you feel an instant connection with. Has that ever happened to you? That dynamic, to keep it in its simplest term, is called immediate social bonding. This type of bonding occurs in other more expected occasions like when you see and hold your newborn for the first time there is lightspeed bonding. Isn't this true? In another occasion, when you meet your soulmate for the first time and within minutes you sense a strong connection deeper than any other that you may have had with anyone else. What begins to develop in this magic moment is an incredible sense of trust, safety, longing, and sentiment that draws the other person closer to you or you to them. The other person gives you access to their world quicker than would happen in a normal, budding relationship of any kind. How can you create a scenario that increases the probability of immediate social bonding or, at the very least, an accelerate feeling of trust and sentiment with another person? There are two ways to achieve this.

One is using simple terms of social endearment and the other is touch. We're going to focus on simple terms of social endearment now and discuss touch in the next chapter. When you consider how words can become powerful tools in creating a greater probability of immediate social bonding there are no more powerful words, in my opinion, than the words "friend" and "brother or sister". These are incredible terms of social endearment. (For those who know me or have spoken with me will attest to the fact that I very often address them as "my friend" or "my brother" or "my sister"). Think about it. When you have someone that you have deemed a friend you have built a relationship of trust, honor, love, care, value, acceptance, and on and on, right? In some cases, it may have taken years of contact and experiences for you to develop a special friendship like that. So, to be called someone's friend holds a special place of esteem and extreme personal value in the eyes and heart of the person addressed. It is not something that is taken lightly in the mind of the hearer or the one being addressed as friend. Are you still with me? Good.

The subconscious mind is also very aware of the word friend. It immediately recognizes the word to mean trusted person. Safe person. Loved person. Fun person. I-can-let-my-guard-down person. Now, remember that the subconscious mind does not judge or analyze data, that is the job of the conscious mind. It only believes and reacts by what it hears, thinks, sees and so on. So, when hearing the word friend, it automatically reacts by sending lightspeed physiological messages that elicit the same feelings that are equivalent to the ones felt when someone is truly called and considered a friend. It doesn't know that you are aren't a true friend. It is up to the conscious mind to analyze the data and determine that call. All the subconscious knows is that they were just called friend. Does this make sense? I hope so because adding the word friend to your communication with someone within the first conversation or second (and certainly ongoing) will give you tremendous advantages. The same can be said about the words "brother" or "sister". These are very intimate terms of endearment as well. Both words elevate the relationship to status of family. A person that I have known my whole life. A person who will love me unconditionally and will always have my back. Someone I can come to in time of need.

Obviously, these are not terms that you would just call anybody unless you have a special relationship that exudes all the attributes just mentioned.

So, to address a new contact by calling them brother or sister has a special effect on the subconscious mind like that of friend. Both terms have a unique way of expressing to the subconscious mind that you are trustworthy, special, safe, a good person, and accepted. Okay, so how do you do this? Well, first you don't complicate such a simple technique. You add the phrase "my friend" or "my brother" or "my sister" to your sentence when addressing someone. That's it! Let the subconscious begin to do its work. Add it as often as you can to your sentence without sounding like a recording and giving off the appearance of being disingenuous. In order words, DON'T OVER DO THIS TECHNIQUE! USE WISDOM. Again, many of you have heard me use, and even address you with, these words. I use them interchangeably in all my conversations when initially meeting someone and even for a while thereafter.

Example of proper uses:

"That's a great question, my friend."

"I'll make sure to get that over to you, my brother."

"What time do you need me there, my sister."

"My friend, can I count on you being there?"

"Hey brother, did I catch you at the right time?"

"So, I was wondering, my friend, what would be the best time for us to meet?"

"My sister, I just want to thank you for your time."

Are you getting this now? Excellent!

WARNING

Do not use this technique if you are on an interview with a potential employer. I don't think your potential boss may appreciate you calling him "brother' on your interview. Similarly, it would not benefit you either if you call a woman "sister" when you are looking to potentially ask her out on a date. Finally, whatever you do, if ever facing a judge, please don't address him as "my friend" ...LOL. Let's move on to touch, shall we?

Technique #3 (Part 2)
"The Subconscious Magic of Touch"

If there were ever medals handed out to the top 3 most powerful ways to immediately change someone's state (even though all 3 would be extremely narrow wins) touch would get the Silver Medal. Subtle or casual touching is a powerful way to make nonverbal communication. This technique, which is also referred as subliminal touching, elicits a subconscious response equally as fast as words do. The difference is that, at times, the response may take a little longer to manifest. However, the duration of manifestation is not really all that important just as long as it does at some point. By the way, in subconscious communication the touch required is a light and subtle touch that is not picked up by the conscious mind (our five faculties of senses) either because it is distracted with other information processing, or it is such a common touch that the conscious mind has been desensitized to it, or simply the conscious mind would never suspect such a touch that it goes undetected. This is the characteristic of anything subliminal.

Again, the conscious mind may not pick up on it, but it doesn't get past the subconscious. It picks it up and must do something with it. The touch I'm referring to is a light pat on the back, a gentle tap on the shoulder, a tap on the arm, and even a "fist bump" works.

Now, think about yourselves for a moment. You become the subject of your own study. What kind of reaction do you have when you've received a "fist bump" or a light tap on your shoulder from another person? I know for me anything like that gives me a sense of connection. I feel comfortable with the person. Can you relate to this as well? This technique is designed to communicate with the subconscious that you can be trusted and are, essentially, a cool person. There have been studies done that have provided further evidence of this very interesting and helpful way to communicate subconsciously.

One such study (The Effect of Counselor Touch in an Initial Counseling Session), documented in the "Journal of Counseling Psychology", female clients that were touched by their counselor during their initial consultation perceived their counselor as significantly more competent than those female subjects who were not touched by the same counselor during their initial consultation. This is a powerful and very telling study for those who engage in initial client or prospect meetings.

Yet, in another study (The Effects of Interpersonal Touch on Restaurant Tipping) published in the "Personality and Social Psychology Bulletin", documented that waitresses who casually touched their customers on the shoulders or hands when returning their change received significantly larger tips that those waitresses who did not.

One last example is found in a study (The Effect of Touch on Women's Behavior) conducted in France as reported in "Social Influence, Psychology Press") documents that there is an increase in compliance when a 1-2 second touch is added to the request. This studied involved young men who, while standing on the street corners, talked to women as they walked by. The study revealed that the men who lightly touched the women's arm while requesting their phone numbers had greater success in getting the phone numbers than those who did not.

WARNING

Subtle or casual touching is very different from grabbing, squeezing, or groping. The latter will send a subconscious message to call the cops or, at very minimum, that you are creepy.

Finally, in the day and age that we live in of sexual harassment and inappropriate advancement and behavior, I must encourage you to use wisdom when applying this technique. Be responsible with its application.

7

Technique #4
"The Incredible…YOU"

There are certain words that can call your subconscious mind to immediate attention and compel it to focus on what is coming next. This is because they force all the subconscious activity and chatter to come to an almost complete halt for a moment. The most powerful of words that accomplish this feat is the word "YOU". The word YOU subconsciously sends the message that I need to be alert and aware of my surroundings because whatever is happening next has to do with my well-being. The highest point of self-awareness is when the other person you are in communication with is addressed with the word YOU. It is as if the subconscious minds say, "Shhh, listen up, this has to do with us".

It is important to remember that the subconscious mind is constantly scanning its surroundings and taking in information and assessing it before it renders judgement and passes it along to the conscious mind for appropriate actions. So, when YOU is received, it will respond accordingly with a heightened alertness to your next set of instructions or directives. It is at the highest susceptible level of compliance. Let me give you an alternate example to drive this point further.

If you have ever been a dog owner or have been around them you know that dogs can be doing what dogs do, then in an instant be at full attention with the owner or someone they're familiar with. Isn't this true? It is almost as if the activity switch gets turned off from whatever they were doing just seconds prior. The moment the owner either calls them, reaches for a treat, gives them a familiar look, or shows them the leash that dog stands at full attention because they know the next set of actions will be about them. It is quite the same with the subconscious mind when it hears the word YOU aimed at it. To put it simply, you have the other person's FULL attention.

The other interesting and advantageous reason why utilizing YOU in your effective communication is the additional subliminal message that it fosters as a result. This is incredibly important for persuasion. When the subconscious mind hears YOU from you, it automatically, begins to attribute credibility from the one who is addressing it. This is paramount for you to understand. The subconscious mind will give you the benefit of the doubt when assessing credibility and whether you are someone of knowledge or importance because you appear to be the one in authority. When you say to another person phrases like, "You really need to hear this"; "I believe in you"; "You are going to thank me for this"; "You are going to excel at this"; "You are going to benefit from this", and so on, it creates an immediate sense of confidence, belief, and trust in the speaker of these words. By the way, all of this is happening at the subconscious level.

Lastly, to achieve maximum results from this technique you must employ repetition. The more you mention the word YOU the more the subconscious mind believes that you are an authority or credible source. It serves to continue convincing or reassuring the other person, at the subconscious level, that you are worthy, valuable, and someone they need to allow to guide them, help them, or simply listen to them. Ultimately, isn't this the end game, anyway? Of course, it is. I knew YOU would get it.

Technique #5
"What's in a name?"

The popular phrase "It's like music to my ears" is often stated when we hear something that is pleasing to our ears, figuratively and literally. Whether it is the sound of a melody, a compliment, good news, the sound of a team winning a major game and so on. It is the acknowledgement of something that has brought you a feeling of relief, comfort, joy, hope, and certainty. We all love to experience that, don't we? Well the one word above all which has the most unique effect on the subconscious mind is your name. That's right. Your name is a precious commodity to you. There is something far more special than just how you are verbally identified or specifically addressed when you are called by your name. Calling someone by their name has far-reaching effects to that person subconsciously more than just getting their attention.

To explore this at a deeper level let's consider that the first name (or oral sounds) that we hear as babies, repetitiously, is our own. As we grow up, hearing the familiar sounds of our name, a subconscious programming begins to take root the more our name (vibrations) is repeated. Now, it is important for me to hit the pause button here for a quick lesson in sound.

A person's name is just a collection of arranged oral sounds which are essentially vibrations fine tuned into a frequency. This frequency is no different than if you were searching for your favorite radio station on the dial. You might think that you are looking for the name of the program but essentially you are tuning into the frequency that your favorite music is playing through. The dial that you select is just the frequency that offers your favorite music. By the way, the reason you stay on that dial after you find it is because the frequency that you've tuned into is bringing something pleasing to you. You still with me? Good.

Returning to my earlier point, we grow up with the familiar frequency embedded in our minds which is our name. It is this programmed frequency that allows for immediate recognition of who we are and begins to generate or return a set of accompanying subtle and subconscious feelings or vibrations. Believe it or not, the sound or speaking of our name has vibrational effects on our subconscious mind. Understanding this, let's piece it together in a way that will help you understand why calling someone's name carries such enormous value in subconscious communication. When you are talking to someone, there is no greater sound or "music to their ears" than their name. The mere sound of their name triggers the exact emotions that you want as you are crafting or positioning your end game or intention for the reason you began communicating in the first place. One of the emotions that surfaces is comfort because of the familiarity and immediate recognition of that sound or frequency. People will, subconsciously, gravitate towards the familiar because of the perceived safety of it and the subconscious mind will always be attracted to what is safe and risk free. When calling someone by their name you are directly telling the subconscious mind that all is well. Another very valuable dynamic that occurs is the feeling of importance that calling someone by their name generates in them. Here's the thing, folks, people want to feel special, important, respected, and valued. We all do, right? Well, there is nothing more effective in helping someone feel this way, subconsciously, than calling them by their name. There is an immediate sense of worth that bubbles up within that person. By the way, when you can make another person feel special, esteemed, respected, and at ease you have someone that will give you far more benefit of the doubt and trust than if you did otherwise.

Another reason why this technique can create for you an exceptional advantage to success in your endeavor is the sense of admiration that the person you are calling feels every time you mention their name. Subconsciously there is a belief that you really admire and respect them. After all, you keep saying their name. Incidentally, the more you say their name the more they begin to feel secure in you and in the possibilities that can lie ahead together. An underpinning sense of hopeful optimism frames a possible future alliance or collaboration. Isn't this the end game? Here, subtle repetition is the tactical key.

Now, keep in mind that this is happening at the subconscious level, so the conscious mind is not rationalizing or analyzing any data here. It is just receiving transmissions from the subconscious mind that says, "I like this person"; "I feel good about this person"; "I could get to know this person"; "I want to be around this person"; "This person appreciates me"; or "This person approves of me". This explains why often you meet someone, and they take an immediate liking to you. You really haven't done much but, unbeknownst to you, you were striking the right frequency keys enough to extract a sense of approval. When there is very little vibrational distortion happening between two people, the result is, a rather quick connection. You can certainly start in the right direction when meeting someone new or fairly new by addressing them by their name as often as logically possible without making it weird.

Finally, this technique serves as a warming component to a new encounter with someone who is a stranger. It acts almost as a sedative to a feeling of resistance that the other person may have when you first meet or speak with them. It allows for the first stroke of a chisel in breaking down the social or relationship wall that many people automatically have as part of their being or personality.

WARNING
Try to NEVER use the person's full name or begin

with Mr. or Ms. Somebody. Why? Simple. Most people have negative memories of times when they were called by their full name or formally. You do not want to conjure up any underlying negative feelings related to times when they were called by their full names. Personally, whenever I was address or called by my full name, it usually meant I was in trouble. The phrase "Mr. Maymi" still puts the fear of God in me. Can you relate to this? When our parents, teachers, or any adults addressed us by our full names, or worse, by Mr. or Ms. Somebody, we knew we were in for it. Somehow things usually didn't end well. Stick with the first name as best you can. This will provide a greater probability of attraction to.

Let me reiterate because I feel I must. Please USE WISDOM with this technique. When it is customary to address someone cordially and formally then you must do so without question.

Lastly, a fun experiment. To prove that this technique works, make it a point that for the next week whenever you meet or see someone wearing a name tag or badge, call them by their name. Do this and watch what happens. You will receive either a smile or a look of surprise that they were addressed by their name. This look of surprise will be followed by a smile or a change in countenance to a much happier and relaxed one. Observe how they treat you from that moment on. Examine the service and attention they'll provide. You will find your test results very encouraging.

9

Technique #6
"Free is Better Than Cheap"

I submit to you that there is a universal human instinct or belief which has existed since the earliest man and is weightier today than ever. That is man's grasp that nothing is truly for free. Everything comes with a cost of some kind. If you ask people from anywhere in the world do they believe that getting something of tremendous value for nothing is realistic or possible most will either say no or be very skeptical at the least. Think about it. How often have we all been offered something for FREE and it really was not free at all? There was a catch to the offer or a small print provision that the free offer was contingent upon. I'm sure you can come up with a few of your own "FREE" stories to fill a chapter in this book, right? So, here is the mystery rub.

If most reasonable and rational thinking people are fairly convinced or skeptical that nothing is truly for free or sincerely comes at no cost or commitment, then why do advertisers, businesses, scammers, even some of our friends, family, co-workers, and so on continue to expound or make offers or claims that something is free? After all, if the masses are seemingly all the wiser about such propositions then wouldn't most attempts to allure people fall flat? It would seem fruitless to even bother, right? Well, not really because what's also widely known is that many people will take a chance on or accept the "FREE" offer. This is why this technique is practiced by every successful marketing or advertising company. It works. People love to hear the words FREE, NO CHARGE, COMPLIMENTARY, and even BUY ONE GET ONE FREE. The subconscious mind responds favorably when it hears these words. Even though the rational thinking mind says, "No way. This can't be free. What's the catch?", the subconscious mind generates the corresponding thoughts and emotions that override the conscious enough for you to say okay to the offer. This explains why you have had your own personal situations when you said yes to an offer even though everything in you was saying "Don't do it. There's a catch." Can you recall such a time or times? Absolutely! It happens to all of us and not just once, either.

By the way, how many times were you right about the catch or about what was also involved in offer? Probably most of the time. So, why do you continue to keep accepting or participating in these offers? Simple. It is very difficult to reprogram the subconscious mind unless you are intent on doing so on such things. In order to fully comprehend this statement, you have to first understand how the subconscious mind process the word FREE or any other similar word or phrase.

When the subconscious mind hears the words

FREE or NO CHARGE, or COMPLIMENTARY it processes them as something that will require very little effort of. It transforms those words to mean that there is very little to lose or get hurt by. In addition, there is hardly any risk that is being taken and nothing is in jeopardy of harm. When these factors are considered the offer is accepted.

An example that many of us are far too familiar with is the "Time Share" experience. This is a classic example of how many people are drawn into time share presentations as a means of accepting free tickets to Disney, a dinner theatre, or a NYC hotel stay. There are countless examples, aren't there? Everyone has their own time share story too. For the record, I'm not knocking time sharing or a time share presentation, but most people who have been through this experience will attest that what they got for "FREE" really cost them more than what they got for free was worth. In fact, time share prospecting and sales tactics are known to be aggressive. So, why is it that those "timeless" time share techniques are still employed today even though the general consensus says, "Stay away from time share people or offers?" Simple answer... it still works! People still get caught up with the FREE stuff even though they are pretty sure that there is probably a catch to it. The word FREE works when triggering the subconscious mind to comply with your request, offer, or invitation. Now, you might be asking, "Then why would anyone say yes when presented with something like this?" People say yes because they know that they can always say no. The subconscious mind gives the green light because it knows that it can always back out. Since, there is no pressure to commit, it presents very little harm or an uncomfortable situation. If it did then the subconscious mind would default to a safe mode and never accept that FREE offer.

This brings me to my final technique.

10

Technique #7
"The Power of Try"

As I mentioned in the previous chapter, people will often be persuaded to comply when the word FREE is embedded in the conversation, advertisement, marketing or some other forum. This is because the word extracts from the subconscious mind another very profound reaction which is integral in effective subconscious communication and that is commitment, or lack thereof. Let's explore this further.

To say that people today are afraid of or hesitant to commit to anything that they cannot back out of at any time is an understatement. It is truly a "test drive" mentality that our society has become accustomed to for the most part. This mentality is alive and well in relationships, job environment, picking schools, doing a business, attending a church, raising a family, marriage, and a bunch more. If you doubt this then begin to observe the number of advertisements that offer "Free Trial Periods", "No Money Down", "Buy Now Pay Later", just to name a few. In fact, in just about every sales or service-driven industry you'll find some form of "no risk" technique being applied. The reason they do this is because they are aware of and have tapped into what we are discussing here. The fact is that people will be more apt to TRY something new or somewhat unfamiliar with as long as it does not produce risk or something uncomfortable for them. This plays right into one of the subconscious mind's attributes which is survival first. Safety first at all cost. Protect the host.

It is worth repeating that the emotions or vibes that the subconscious mind transmits to the conscious mind when it senses the possibility of being hurt is hesitation, fear, and doubt. Keep in mind that the subconscious mind has stored memory of past experiences of failure, pain, and discomfort and any mere indication of another such episode occurring again is shot down immediately. So, incorporating the word TRY in your dialogue will have amazing effects simply because it soothes the subconscious mind with a sense of safety. If you continue to provide encouraging words that will further relieve any concern of pain or discomfort, then you will be more successful in your communication efforts.

Additionally, when a person is encouraged by a good friend, respected organization, or valued person to TRY, the probability of compliance increases because as trust increases fear decreases. Are you getting this? Returning to the earlier point, with a "test drive" mindset that we are living in the word TRY (or any similar phrase) relays to the subconscious mind that they can "un-try" at any time or bail out because there is no die-hard commitment required. They are not going to be locked into something they cannot get out of. They will not experience difficulty or discomfort if they decide to not continue moving forward. In other words, easy in – easy out. This is music to the ears of the subconscious mind, figuratively speaking, of course. Finally, the subconscious mind does not do change too well. In fact, it is quite resistant to it because, not only, does it require repetitive effort, but it means completely reprogramming old habits, behaviors, and beliefs that are deep rooted, comfortable, and very familiar. Therefore, upon processing the idea of trying it recognizes that there is no threat to or promise to change anything. This plays extremely well into our current social mindset.

CLOSING

It is my sincerest hope that you will find this work extraordinarily useful and advantageous in your pursuit of communication effectiveness and overall success in all of your endeavors, my friend.

If you purchased this book it is because YOU are a very special person who is hungry to succeed. Let me encourage you to IMAGINE what life will look like for you when you begin to master the utilization of these techniques effortlessly. The WONDERFUL NEW ASSOCIATIONS WITH PEOPLE that you will begin to make will add untold value to your life and business experience. I can promise you that it will COST YOU NOTHING to TRY but everything if you don't.

(Did you like the beautiful arrangements of words above? Did you catch the words I used? Nice, huh? I swear if you had been standing next to me, I probably would have subtly touched you too.) LOL!

ABOUT THE AUTHOR

Founder of Survive to Thrive Marketing (**www.survivetothriveguide.com**)
Purveyor of The Jay Maymi - "Don't just survive...Thrive!" (**www.thejaymaymi.com**)
Keynote Speaker for the National Speaker Association (**www.nsa.org**)
Creator of "Survive to Thrive TV"

Author of "A Common Man's Devotional", "The Entrepreneur's Devotional", "Survive to Thrive – A Guide for the New Network Marketer", "The Prospecting Survival Guide" (Vols. 1 & 2), and "Recruiting Mastery".

A WORD FROM JAY MAYMI

"There is an advantage to growing up in a humble setting with meager means. The reality of your circumstances can either pummel you into mediocrity or extract from you a burning desire to excel and rise above. My story is one of the latter. For the last three decades my hunger to rise above has yielded an impressive array of accomplishments. From multiple successful businesses to bodybuilding championships, radio, TV, stage, and print work to authoring 5 books; from an entire Sales and Personal Development series to speaking in front of many diverse audiences on different topics; all have uniquely qualified me to offer valuable knowledge, instruction, inspiration, and impact to those seeking to develop a higher and greater expression of themselves."

BE SURE TO SUBSCRIBE TO THESE PORTALS FOR MORE RESOURCES AND TRAINING:

Survivetothriveguide.com

Youtube.com/c/JayMaymiSurvivetoThrive

Facebook.com/survivetothrivebiz

@THEJAYMAYMI

More books from Jay Maymi

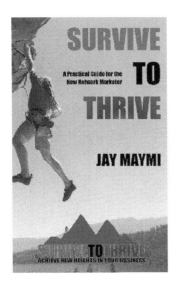
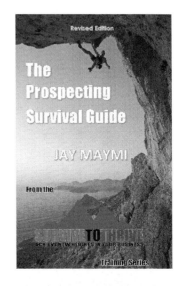
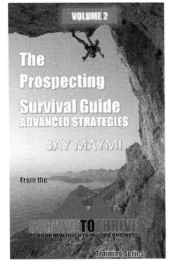

Available at **www.survivetothriveguide.com**

Made in the USA
Middletown, DE
01 February 2019